I0471409

SEO Training Manual - The 10 Golden Steps To Shower In Search Engine Traffic

by Dan Moskel
http://www.danmoskeluniversity.com

Copyright 2013 - All Rights Reserved

ISBN-13:
978-1492816256

ISBN-10:
1492816256

Dan Moskel - In Person

Dan Moskel wants to work with YOU & speak with your church group, sales organization, school, and local business!

If you have a BRILLIANT shark tank idea or just need some additional help with your online business ... we would love to hear from you!

For more contact us at:
Dan Moskel
email: dmoskel@gmail.com
http://www.danmoskeluniversity.com

Table of Contents

What Is Search Engine Optimization?

This is how you can get FREE, natural, and organic search traffic from Google, Yahoo, and Bing. This does NOT require you to spend 7 figures in advertising, as I personally did for many years.

This doesn't mean you should stop doing paid advertising if your currently are, but this is an investment of time versus money. And thus much more ideal for folks with a shoestring or no advertising budget to get started.

In this brief report I am going to walk you through and train you in my methods of adding new content to your website in order to get this VALUABLE real-estate of organic, natural, free listings and traffic!

Justin Bieber and Me

The short idea is SEO (search engine optimization) is just like high school. You want to make sure you are hanging out with Justin Bieber and Zach Morris from

Saved by the Bell and your website is not like SCREECH or Steve Urkel.

The authority, amount of content, number of friends and links will determine your internet popularity and thus where you website will rank in the organic search results.

Is Google a Zoo Keeper?

If you are new to SEO or have seen your world turned upside down after all the Google zoo keeper updates, your on the right path moving forward with SEO in 2014 if your focus is now on your website content.

Below I have laid out the simple 7 steps to add new content for SEO purposes. Many of the techniques of the past are gone and dead, and the reality is many websites are now being notified of 'spammy' inbound link building … this results in negative SEO.

*** In other words, STOP building inbound links from other websites like article directories, blog networks, directory websites, using automation tools, etc. … you are doing more harm than good for your website!

The magical world of SEO that Google preached way back in 2006 is finally a reality. The search engines have become sophisticated enough that "internet utopia" is here and going to continue as the gods intended.

Your focus should now be 95% on your website and on page optimization with only 5% spent building links from trusted sites like social media.

What Is SEO Content ... Really?

SEO content is information and articles about related and similar subject material.

The idea is that you are building out your website and giving yourself a bigger claim of real estate by showing the search engines that you are a reliable, authoritative, and trustworthy website with a lot of helpful information.

Step 1 - Choose your BULLSEYE TARGET

Before you write a word you need to choose a target.

This is just like when you get in the car to go somewhere. You don't leave the house without a destination in mind!

You should do some keyword research to identify your bullseye.

For example if you are creating a website and adding content to claim real-estate within the credit repair niche.

Your website will have an impossible task to rank for the term 'credit repair' if you only have 4 pages on your website.

Continuing with this example 'credit repair' could be your big picture and home page target.

If so, your next article topics could be

- Do-it-yourself credit repair
- Legal credit repair
- Online credit repair
- Bad credit repair
- Professional credit repair

It will also help immensely to have other sub-topic and related pages.

For instance:

- How to improve your credit score
- How to build credit
- How to remove bad credit
- How to dispute your credit report

*** But, you would NOT want your next pages to be chocolate chip cookie recipes, dating advice, or how to write a book … IT IS TOTALLY UNRELATED.

You want to build out upon topics and subjects. You website will evolve!

How To Do Your Research?

YOU MUST USE A RELIABLE keyword tool to help you discover what topics, subjects, and exact keywords are being searched and how often.

You want to target terms that are searched for with a good volume of searches per month.

You would not want to target a term if it is only searched 4 times a month, if you could target a term that is instead searched for 4,000 times or 40,000 times.

Where To Get This Information

There are a number of keyword tools available. I suggest and personally use the recently moved Google keyword tool it is now called the Google Keyword Planner.

You will have to create Google AdWords account if you do not already have one, and their are other free tools you can use but I recommend using Googles Keyword Planner for your research.

This will provide you with the most accurate volume per month.

In other words, how often different keyword terms are searched within Google, every month.

If folks are searching in Google for terms you can assume they are searching Yahoo and Bing exactly the same term.

However, Google has more of the search market so Yahoo and Bing will not provide as much volume. With that said they do have a BIG piece of the market and can give you some great traffic to your site!

Once you identify your target keyword term, write it down. I would also suggest that you use the Google Keyword Planner and check the exact match type.

This is the best indicator as to exactly what people are typing in and searching for in Google. There is also broad and phrase match option in the Keyword Planner.

You may want to compare these to get the best idea, I typically focus on exact match.

How Much Volume?

Generally speaking, you should target keyword terms with a minimum of 100 monthly searches using exact match and there is no maximum number of searches.

But, we must caution you that using the earlier example 'credit repair' it would take a new website years to rank on the first page for that term.

This is because it is an UBER competitive niche market with most all other sites targeting that term.

Instead, use that keyword term, as a big picture goal and focus on the less competitive and long tail keyword terms.

There are endless subjects within this general topic that you can focus your immediate efforts on while working toward your big picture goal.

Including:

- Bad credit
- Negative items on your credit report
- Late payments
- Credit card charge offs
- Defaulted student loans
- Credit bureaus
- Identity theft
- Apply for a mortgage
- Car loans with bad credit

And all the subjects we mentioned earlier, plus many more!

This is true of every industry and if it isn't true of your niche, you need to go back to the drawing board and broaden your horizon.

It will be much easier to get ranked for and get traffic to your website on the less competitive keyword terms.

Doesn't this sound better than to fight in the center of the bull ring?

Why not take the easier path and collect all the coins from outside the center of the ring?

<u>There are a lot less bulls to fight!</u>

This has been my general strategy since 2006, with great success on all types of terms. Including, super competitive keyword terms.

The idea is you are working smart. Think in terms of return on your time investment.

I think you would rather give yourself a smaller raise today, and again tomorrow, and the day after … compared to hoping for a big raise on respectfully a bit of a pipe dream!

For this example specifically there are websites that have been doing SEO for a decade and longer!

That is how far behind a new website is, doesn't mean it can't happen but you first have to get the smaller terms.

I could go into much more detail but just make sure you have a reasonable expectation of what you really want.

I want money, and I hope you do too!

Hit the easy spots ... there truly are some GOLD MINES! And always overlooked sections in every market and industry!

Watch what works and keep trying and keep building!

This is the most valuable SEO advice you can receive especially post zoo keeper updates. It is most relevant and valued by the search engines if you do correctly.

Step 2 - Create Your Search Snippet

What is your snippet? Great question. :)

This is what shows up in the search results for your website. And is the image below.

Credit Help — Answers For Your Credit Questions

www.yourbadcreditcard.net/ ▾
by Dan Willis
Get help with your bad credit and credit repair questions. We provide easy to understand articles in hopes to help your credit concerns.

Use the metaphor that your snippet is just like an advertisement. You want to get attention, interest, and visitors to your website.

Test different headlines, descriptions, everything. And see what produces results.

Google and the other search engines do factor in you CTR or click-thru-rate. Or how often your website gets clicked on versus the website below you and above you.

You want a GOOD click through rate.

Your snippet is made up of your title tag (headline), meta description, url address, and for our snippet we added Google authorship to show our picture.

Let's talk about how best to create your advertisement, snippet, website traffic grabber.

Headline ... Title Tag

The very top shows up in blue in the search engines, it is your headline and 'Title Tag' in SEO geek speech.

Your headline is the title of your article. It should be keyword rich, attention getting, compelling, and be a bullseye on your keyword target term.

You will have 70 characters in Google for your title. If you write more it will result in a ... showing up.

Let's use an example and then talk about why this is so important.

For a page where we are targeting the keyword term: 'dispute credit report'

We have listed 4 example titles below, you select which one you believe is best and we will discuss.

1. Dispute Credit Report

2. How To Dispute Credit Report Information

3. Dispute Credit Report - 7 Mistakes

4. The 5 Steps To Dispute Credit Report Errors

I recommend you experiment with your title but this is the first thing people see that will determine if they click and visit your website.

If you said #3 or #4 that is what I would choose, today. People like lists, they like steps, how to is good as well.

Try different things and see what works best.

Think

Think ... if you were trying to file a credit report dispute what title would speak the most to you?

Put yourself in the searchers shoes. And think in terms of what they want.

This is also important because your headline will most directly influence your CTR (click through rate).

It makes sense for the search engines to use your CTR as a ranking factor. If website x is getting clicked twice as often as website y.

We could assumer website x has better information.

There are many other factors including how long that individual spends on your website but having a good click thru is very important!

Meta Description

The meta description is the two sentences below your website title.

The headline gets their attention and then your two sentence summary describes your content. This is limited to 156 characters. If you write more it will show up as ...

Using the #4 headline or title above a good description would be:

"Avoid these 7 deadly sins when disputing your credit report and find out how you can erase damaging errors from your credit history."

* On a side it can help your page target synonym keyword terms and related terms like disputing credit report, if you use these terms in your meta description and URL address. With this example we used 'disputing credit report' in our description and we could use the URL address of example.com/credit-report-dispute

This way we are targeting the keyword term 'dispute credit report' in the title, "disputing credit report" in the description, and 'credit report dispute' with the URL address.

We are giving ourself a chance to rank for related high volume search terms along with setting a laser target to rank for the keyword term dispute credit report.

This is slightly advanced and you should not spend extra time to do this. Just as you become more comfortable with SEO and have some experience then, expand and test these more advanced approaches.

URL Address

In the past more micro sites with keyword terms in their URL address were given value like 'disputecreditreport.com' but today according to reports that is no longer true …

However what is still valued by Google is what you place after your website.com/_____

You should include '-' hyphens to separate words and try to keep it short. To clarify your new page should have a similar URL as:

http://www.website.com/keword-target-term-here

Be cautious, make sure you don't publish an existing URL address on your website.

In other words don't publish two pages with the same URL address because only one page will be available. It's a mistake I have personally made and on par with shooting yourself in the foot. :)

You Created Your Snippet

That's it. This information is your snippet or ad for your website page.

Step 3 - Internal Website Links

Before you publish a new page. You must go through and make sure you add a few internal website links.

This is linking to other related pages on your website. You must also choose good anchor text for these internal website links.

Anchor text is the hyperlinked word that shows up in a different color and when it is clicked on will take you to another web page.

You should again use a keyword tool to help you choose the anchor text for your internal links.

The idea is when you use an internal link you are casting a vote to the search engines that you other webpage is about the anchor text keyword term.

And you are telling the search engines that your other page should show up for that specific search term. This is the keyword term that you used as your anchor text.

For example:

With our page about how to dispute your credit report it would be VERY smart for us to make an internal link on the next webpage we create.

And on the new page link to the dispute credit report page with the keyword term: 'dispute credit report'

This is EXACTLY like inbound links of the past.

You want to choose popular search terms and use synonyms. Avoid using the exact same anchor text for every single internal link over to a specific page.

Instead you need to vary and use the popular searched keyword terms and synonyms from time to time.

It will also help your search optimization with some occasional internal links to your home page, and category pages.

In a general sense you want to internally link to your most important pages. The pages that are your immediate goals to get traffic.

How Often?

You should use internal linking roughly every 150 words. With that said, the more internal links you have the less they will count.

The same value is divided between all your internal links on a new webpage.

This means you will have an extra mouth to feed with each internal link on your page.

We suggest you try different approaches but the less links the more weight and value each will be given and pass along through your internal links to your important pages.

Step 4 - Format Your Content To Be User and Search Engine Friendly

You need to spend a minute and make sure you have uniform formatting on your website content.

It looks strange from a human perspective and a search engine perspective, if you have different font size, colors, types on different pages. Try to keep it all exactly the same.

For my website I use Verdana font at 14 point. And specifically with my WordPress design I have to manually change the font color to black on all new pages.

Additionally you want to think about the user experience when they land on your website.

This relates to showing a big massive sized text block or a single sentence that looks easy to read.

The reality is many people will skim your content, so make it easy for them to skim over it.

If it is then they will be more likely to fully read it and consume your information.

For me when I see massive text blocks on a website I go to the next site instantly.

I strongly suggest very short sentences.

The average American reads on a 6th grade level, so write with the intention of understanding rather than trying to remember what your 9th grade English teacher said about sentence structure!

As Milo Frank says:

"Only someone who truly knows his subject can say what he wants to say in clear and simple language."

You want people to understand your message. It is the MOST IMPORTANT thing to communicating!

Spacing is key to, the more white space you have, the friendlier it is to visitors of your website. I often write in one sentence paragraphs.

I just find it easier to consume information that way, it is easy to look at and easy to read.

I am vehemently opposed to even the idea of reading six sentences with no spaces!

Biggest Mistake to Avoid

I've worked with many, many, many folks over the years. And the biggest, most common mistake I see is putting two spaces after a period.

word. start of next sentence.

word. start of next sentence.

It is only one space! I'm not sure if this two spaces comes from formal schooling, despite my 10 year undergraduate path. But, it does not apply to your website and online content!

It's possible that if you paste content you wrote in Microsoft Word or another word processor that they formatting gets messed up.

If you paste content in, I strongly suggest making it 'plain text format.'

I do this in notepad and then paste the content into my website. Then go through bolding, underling, formatting tweaks.

Step 5 - Review Your Content

PLEASE, PLEASE, PLEASE review your content to make sure your information is on topic.

I have personally found that often it makes sense to tweak my title, headline or to rearrange an article before I publish it.
Your goal is to give people the exact information they want up front!

Then at the end of your article you can include other relevant information such as why it's important to dispute incorrect listings on your credit report, the brick walls, or why your service or product can benefit people looking for this information.

Again think in terms of your user!
Answer the initial search question in the

very first part of your article, regardless of the topic.

If you don't do this, people will skip to the next website and you won't have a chance to talk about your product, service, or any other message anyway!

Step 6 - Don't
OVER-THINK

Listen, you have a lot of information to consider with SEO and creating additional content.

Don't over-think it!

You can always edit it later. That is one BIG benefit to working online.

Also, for SEO purposes you will get a much bigger reward and more traffic if you create more content.

Don't try to write a 'perfect' article instead aim for excellence and write more articles. The more you do the easier it becomes. You will make mistakes, that I guarantee!

Laugh at your mistakes. And your earlier writing. Earl Nightingale says it best that when he looks at his writing from 10 years ago he sees how much better it could be. This means he has GROWN and gotten better, more skilled, and talented as a writer ... THIS SHOULD BE YOUR GOAL TOO!

Step 7 - Go For It and Press Publish

When you have hit your good enough point, publish the darn article!

This book is about content marketing as in you had better publish a lot of content to get the most benefit from this training.

Don't stress mistakes, instead aim for excellence.

And remember to grow and get better with every article and writing project you take on.

You can do GREAT! I have FAITH in you! If you pay the price you will be adequately rewarded! And get a golden shower of free, natural, organic traffic!

Step 8 - Inbound Links Post SEO Algorithm Updates

When it comes to SEO your inbound links are some of the most important indicators to the search engines and their algorithms when ranking your website.

As a result of many search algorithm updates over the years, inbound links are now viewed much differently.

Now, the quality of the website that links to your website is of crucial importance. It still remains true that the anchor text for your inbound link will help you rank for that specific search term.

Let's use an example to fully illustrate this. If a reputable website such as CNN were to give your website an inbound link using the anchor text "financial advice."

Then the search engines would view your website as being about "financial advice" and you would be more likely to rank for the term "financial advice" than a website without an inbound link from CNN.

Because CNN is a trusted authority an inbound link from their website to your website will be given a a lot of value.

In years past, it was your responsibility as a webmaster to go out and build inbound links to your website. This was the primary way of getting traffic and optimizing your site for the search engines.

According to Matt Cutts of Google, these old inbound linking strategies such as article marketing, are no longer given as much value.

In fact, if you have spammy websites giving you inbound links, you could see your rankings suffer.

Within the Google webmaster tools some folks are being notified of what appears to be spamming and unnatural inbound links.

This is happening when Google believes you are going out and building inbound links to your site.

As SEO was initially intended an inbound link was supposed to be viewed as an editorial choice.

In other words, other websites would provide you with an inbound link to your website because you have good, quality, and helpful information.

While your inbound links still hold value in today's search algorithms, there has been a dramatic shift over the past few years.

It is of equal, perhaps even more importance that you provide good on page optimization. This includes your page title, meta-descriptions, internal linking, and most importantly the content of your website.

If you want to rank for the keyword term "financial advice" then you had better have good content about financial advice. In addition, you should have a number of related articles on subjects within that niche.

For instance, you should add related pages topic's such as saving for retirement, 401(k), even getting out of debt.

On the other hand, you should not create pages about chocolate chip cookies or other irrelevant subject matter. This is true with inbound links as well.

If your target keyword term is "financial advice" your website will benefit more from and inbound link from CNN as opposed to the Food Network website.

The size of your website, the related information you provide, along with inbound links, social media signs, and many other factors contribute to how well your website performs with search results.

I would encourage you to follow my practices of no longer building inbound links except from social media outlets.

I have received notice from Google webmaster tools that have indicated sections of one of my websites as been penalized for the appearance of unnatural link building.

To clarify and sum this up search engine optimization has become advanced enough to finally practice what they preached for so many years.

Avoid using article marketing, automated link building programs, blog networks, and any other unnatural ways to build inbound links.

With today's algorithm you are more likely to hurt your rankings and penalize your site by building links than help it. Let SEO work the way it was intended and let other websites give you an editorial choice for an inbound link.

You should instead invest your energy into building pages on your website with good on page SEO and use internal linking with good anchor text to help your best pages and website as a whole rank better in the search results.

Step 9 - The 2 Most Common Questions and Expectations for Beginners to SEO

1. Ranking fluctuations

The search algorithms are always changing. If you see your website move up a few spots or down a few spots it could just be due to the search algorithms changing.

2. Overnight #1 ranking

Some of the very highly competitive terms will take weeks, months, years to ever get ranked for.

Instead, we would suggest new smaller websites start with easier terms and keep the super competitive terms as big picture goals for their site.

It will be easier to get ranked and traffic for less competitive terms and thus newer websites should start with easier and more realistic goals to get traffic.

Step 10 - Your 7 Point SEO Checklist for New Website Content

Below is your 7 point SEO checklist when it comes to good search engine optimization for your new content.

These pieces of information you have direct control over. You should use them to help get your website natural, free, and organic search traffic.

1. Headline

This is also the title of your new post, page, article. This should describe what your article is about.

Your headline should also target the keyword search term. I would suggest using the Google Keyword Tool to help you find high volume search terms to target with your new content.

In addition, your headline should try to be attention-getting. If you can write a compelling headline that will get your page clicked on often. Then, your page should benefit by getting more traffic.

2. Description

This is about 2 sentences and what your specific web page is about. It is going to show up directly below the title in the search engine results.

Again use some direct marketing tools to help engage searchers and get them to click on your website. The CTR (click-thru-rate) or how often your website gets clicked on is a signal the search engines use when ranking your site.

3. Length

I would suggest that your article be a minimum of 500 words. It appears to me that the search engines are favoring longer content.

I would encourage you to go all out and make your article as long as it needs to be, within reason. If your over 2,000 words you may want to consider splitting it into two articles.

It would be smart to avoid writing thin or shallow content. Make sure that you have some opinion or personal view in your articles.

Avoid regurgitating product ad specs. This is specifically to avoid having a thin website which will not get much love from the search engines!

4. URL Address

This is of less importance but try to include your search keyword or a variation of that keyword in your URL address. This is just one more signal that your new webpage has relevant information about your target keyword term.

5. Internal Linking

In the past the search engines used to value good anchor text for your back links. This same view is now true with your internal linking and the anchor text you use. From my experience.

These are all links that point to other pages on your website. If you choose good anchor text the actual words that hyperlink and typically show up in blue as popular search terms. Then your website should benefit tremendously.

I can speak firsthand to how important and powerful good internal linking is, and taking a moment to choose good anchor text. Doing this well can REALLY leverage your site.

I've been able to use it to get first page search rankings on very competitive terms. Your voting for yourself and your own website, and you should! Google in my opinion encourages you to do this.

On a side with internal linking reports suggest you do this no more than every 100-150 words. If you had an article of 600 words then you would only use 4 internal links.

The more weight will be given each link with fewer internal links on your page.

The value will be dispersed among all the links on your new webpage so if you have 20 internal links it won't mean much. However if instead, you have only 3 links it will be valued highly.

6. Outbound Links

If it is relevant or appropriate for a page to include an outbound link, DO IT! By linking out from your website to trusted authorities even government agencies when it is appropriate. It will help your site and give it more credibility.

For example:

On this page we included an outbound link to the Google Keyword Tool, because it is a good tool. We would encourage you and our friends, and family to use this, we do.

If you have appropriate outbound links it will make your website appear more credible, trustworthy, and authoritative. It just makes sense to have some outbound links when making a website!

7. Call To Action

When readers get to the bottom of your article make sure you include a call to action. You can ask your readers to go check out your related articles, to sign up for your newsletter, get a free consultation, etc.

Tell your readers if you write your own book like our recent publication titled How To Create a Website Easy Button available at Amazon.

You can also use this to help plug really important articles on your website such as our guide to affiliate marketing for beginners.

Special Free Gift From The Author

Copy this page and send it to:
Dan Moskel
1045 Mineral Creek Ct.
Lexington, SC 29073

Currently we are performing free SEO reviews for members in our 'Top-Secret SEO Circle' if you would like to join this insiders group and stay ahead of the curve ACT NOW!!

And get a limited time FREE BONUS ... Dan Moskel will personally review your website, create a unique SEO plan, and provide you a free 30 minute phone consultation to help implement your one-of-a-kind plan for more traffic, more leads, more sales, and most importantly more MONEY!

There is a one-time charge of $29.95 to join and get this FREE BONUS SEO ACTION PLAN from Dan Moskel and you have no obligation to continue at the lowest Gold Membership price of $19.95 per month ($29.95 outside North America). In fact, should you continue with Membership, you may later cancel at any time.

Name

_____

Business Name

_____

Address

_____

_____

_____

City, State, Zip

_____

_____

_____

Business __   Home __

E-Mail

_____

Fax

_____

Phone

_____

__ American Express

__ Visa

__ MasterCard

Card#

_____

Exp Date

_____

Signature

_____

Date

_____

Providing this information constitutes your permission for Dan Moskel to contact you regarding information via above listed means.

www.ingramcontent.com/pod-product-compliance
Lightning Source LLC
Chambersburg PA
CBHW051224170526
45166CB00005B/2032